PRISON IS
NOT FOR ME

PRISON IS
NOT FOR ME

WILLIAM S. GREENE

About the Book

A book that every parent of a developmentally disabled person should read.... This book was written to alert all people working in the law enforcement and judicial field to be aware and recognize disabilities and not mistake them for criminal behavior....

ACKNOWLEDGEMENTS

So many people were unimpressed and disinterested when I stated that I would write a book about P.C. 1370.1 that giving credit to those who paid attention at all is easy and not very lengthy.

To my talented and very interested editor, Lange Winckler, I must pay a tribute of special note. Lange is not merely a valued friend but a kindred soul with the same special reasons for wanting to see this book completed.

In the same category is Martha Sillman, whom some have regarded as 'too militant' in a cause which abounds with timid souls. She saw the need and encouraged it and me.

Jerry and Susan Gould quietly and calmly told me that the project was quite necessary. They knew why. So did many of the people in L.A. Goal.

And I must acknowledge the many writers, researchers and editors who provided me with grist for the mill of voluminous notes ... even if the greatest amount went unused.

DEDICATION

I dedicate this labor of love to a friend and relative who wishes his name not to be mentioned … and to devilish Janet … as well as to all in this world who love and care for them.

PREFACE

A few months ago I received a phone call from someone asking me if "Prison Is Not For Me" is still in print and where can one obtain a copy. A speaker had recommended the book as necessary reading for all parents of the developmentally disabled.

I was surprised. First of all because the book has been our of print for so many years, and secondly because I wasn't certain the information it contained was still valid.

So I re-read my own copy and was amazed at how relevant the facts in "Prison Is Not For Me" remain. Not only do we have police testifying as to their erroneous perceptions in the Rodney King case, but in spite of TV writers' attempts to portray their developmentally disabled characters sympathetically, prejorative and offensive terms referring to them slip into the language of scripts much too often without regard to the emotional jolts they give to the thusly disabled themselves and those who love them most.

Be that as it may, it is difficult to determine how much progress has been made in the field. Especially by one who has lived with the situation for so long and has faced new and different problems as each year passes.

"Prison Is Not For Me" is an awareness project. It was and is still intended to make the grocery checker,. the security guard, the ticket taker, the teacher, the bus driver and everyone who may come in contact with a Charlie or Janet or Mark or Hazel, recognize with whom he or she is dealing.

Not designed to be a medical or a legal treatise or a how-to-book or a morality story, the book is a condensed and concise version of an initial two hundred and forty pages of a more comprehensive attempt to cover the subject matter. Without sacrificing the depth and meaning of the content, I edited it down to the most pertinent and poignant aspects of my own perceptions without pendantry or maukish sentimentality. The result became a sixty page lean and meaningful attempt at awareness heightening. The only negative review of the book was a comment by the Los Angeles Times writer who said it was too small to qualify as a book, admitting however that it did make its point.   The California Supreme Court reversed the conviction of a retarded boy's criminal conviction wherein "Prison Is Not For Me" was quoted in an Amicus Brief in support of the reversal.[*]

Yet there's only enough law in the book on need-to-know level for parents and those similarly involved; just so much explanation of the roles one should play as appears absolutely necessary to protect our special folks…

And my son Charles is 35 years old now.

Institutions I mention have not been all I had hoped they would be.   But they are still around.   And, alas, although I have devoted my concern and devotion to my son, I did not devote my whole life to the 'cause'.   New generations of parents are now around with their own ideas and energies.   I hope this very concise and concept packed volume may help them.   Especially in spreading awareness.

William S. Greene

5/1992

[*] In Ramon M. (1976)

FIRST EDITION COMMENTS

As this book goes to press, two significant events are taking place. California's Governor Jerry Brown signed into law a measure which will, among other things, diminish the stigma of labelling developmentally disabled (retarded), people. And the legal profession is discussing problems of our children much more consistently.

Thus, this book appears in print at a most appropriate moment in the events of men.

On a personal note, my thoughts about writing tended to lean toward those works of greatness in literature. "Prison Is Not For Me" is motivated by more impelling and demanding stuff than an ephemeral search for The Great American Novel.

Help is needed. I am responding to that ever-growing need.

Mentally-disabled, brain-damaged citizens range from the entirely helpless to those whose mild impairments lead them to eventually blend into society and disappear as individual standouts or a class. But ... they are nevertheless around. And they are nevertheless vulnerable to the ignorance, bigotry or misguided mischievousness of others.

'Prison Is Not For Me' is an attempt to give direction to the many who care and are interested when a disabled person of the kind mentioned above finds himself or herself in the dilemma of legal jeopardy that P.C. 1370.1 is designed to deal with.

I am proud to reside in and be part of the beautiful and innovative State of California which made 1370.1 part of its Penal Code. California has led the nation and the world in so many fine things. This legal measure is a great step forward.

I trust that the readers of this book will find the inspiration and adventure which I found from the time I first was invited to add my views to inception of Section

1370.1 PC, to this day, when I hope my further efforts will put into practice the effective use of a good law.

William S. Greene

Granada Hills, California

October, 1976

CHAPTER ONE

PUNISHMENT WITHOUT CRIME

Crime does not come easily to a retarded person, or to a developmentally disabled individual. Among the many reasons for this are the innocence of the retarded, the inhibitions of trust and belief in authority that we "normal" adults can dispense with by mean of our "superior" reasoning powers, and, finally, the fear of retribution for wrongdoing.

But there is a more fundamental reason that crime as we know it is not commonplace with the retarded—crime, *as we know it*, often does not exist.

For example, when a group of playing children, aged two to six or seven, indulge in the natural sexual playing exhibited at those ages, we do not consider this to be "crime." Perhaps some parents, unable to cope with sexuality, severely punish the innocent curiosity of children—but no police are called, no judges asked to rule on the future incarceration of the playful children.

But many fearful adults demand "protection for society" If a retarded person—regardless of age—is accused of similar innocent curiosity.

"Crime" is a relative concept. To be humane, the law must include in its relative definitions of crime and punishment acknowledgement of the needs and rights of the retarded. Perhaps, as one study points out, the retarded or developmentally disabled commit fewer crimes per capita than "normal" people, but still, another study points out that a disproportionate number of imprisoned persons are considered retarded. Both studies tell us the need for a system of law, enforcement, and administration with room for the retarded as a minority class.

The stories that follow show the contrast between "ordinary" administration of justice, and operation of the law under California's Penal Code Section 1370.1, which acknowledges the special needs of the retarded and/or developmentally disabled. In the case of the second illustration, a true story, the attorney and parent involved were fortunate to understand this little-known section of law and put it to work.

As the following pages unfold, we will see how other concerned laymen and professionals can themselves make use of this law for the benefit of society and the retarded.

Putting Peter Away

"Please, I haven't done anything wrong. Don't take me away. Prison is not for me—please!"

Although he could not understand quite what he had been accused of, Peter knew all too well what was happening to him. He was being placed in "jail," actually a high-security state hospital, and taken from his mother and father. At 19, Peter was known to be retarded, but he had learned much in his short life, from friends, family, books, television, and school—and one of the most important lessons he had learned was that his parents loved him—while "jail" was a bad place for bad people.

Peter was pleading with uniformed officers of the court which had ordered him committed following an insistent campaign by a liberal, warmhearted schoolteacher who felt she had to "protect society from dangerous people." While Peter's name is false, this story of tragic coldness in the law is sadly true.

Peter's only crime was the normal sexual exploration with a neighborhood playmate which children undertake. Peter, although a man in years, was about nine intellectually. The mother of the girl, 14 and quite mature, discovered the two in their embarrassing exposure—and the schoolteacher, a neighbor, later heard the story and decided she had to do something about it.

The parents of both children felt there was no reason to make anything of what was a decidedly minor incident. The teacher insisted that "justice be done," that "this dangerous boy" be reported to proper authorities.

The girl's parent dismissed her neighbor's pleadings; the parents of the retarded boy begged the teacher to drop her crusade, that the boy had never before caused anyone any problems, that there was no reason to put him away.

An obsession grew out of the teacher's initial concerns that she do something about a problem in the neighborhood. She badgered the girl's parents enough that they finally went to the city attorney and lodged a complaint. The boy's parents begged the playmate's family to drop the prosecution, pointing out that a normal boy would not be hounded in this way.

In her wisdom, the teacher admitted that if one of her boys had done something similar (and she said it is certain they had, but were not discovered at it), the response would be different. "But a retarded boy is dangerous."

Under the law at the time of this incident, the boy was put through a terrible ordeal with his parents before he was finally committed to an institution. The teacher didn't hear the young man defending his innocence as he was torn from his family and life: "Please, don't take me away. Prison is not for me!"

When this incident occurred, California Penal Code Section 1370.1, did not exist. Had it been in force and recognized by the family or court, the outcome might have been very different.

Yet even today, with the existence of 1370.1, the potential for a repeat of this story remains. Far too few jurists, defense and prosecuting attorneys, and members of the public, recognize the existence and purpose of the law.

Consider the outcome of a similar event—also true—when a parent, judge attorney, and mental health professional all worked together under the terms of 1370.1 in the face of determined efforts by police and prosecution to commit a retarded young man to an institution:

Hope for Hollis

Hollis, a retarded young man who is intellectually at the third-grade level, was accused by another neighborhood boy of a crime. He is not accused directly, but notified by a special Section of the police department that complaint has been lodged against him. Because of the nature of the crime he is not immediately arrested.

Hollis' father, an attorney active in legal representation of the retarded, faces a problem: His son has denied the charge, and deserves vindication in court, as well as justice done in a civil suit against those who have brought the false charge against his child. He would also prefer to avoid the rigors of a trial by bringing proceedings under Section 1370.1 PC and completely blocking actions to determine guilt or innocence.

The father decides to take his son to the police station for an interrogation, to see if officers will recommend filing of charges by the prosecutors. At this point Hollis' father serves also as his attorney.

Sure his son will vindicated, the father waives his "client's" Fifth Amendment rights and permits the questioning. The police officer in the case presses hard: Hollis steadfastly denies the allegations, showing horror that he would be accused of homosexual advances toward a neighbor's son. It is painful for the father to see his son suffer under the pressure.

Instead of resulting in dropping of the matter and an end to the ordeal, Hollis' interrogation concludes with a request for photographing. A standard police tactic to determine if a suspect is possibly involved in other crimes, the unspoken alternative to the request is immediate booking for arraignment on the charges. From this, Hollis' father knows it is evident the police will recommend filing charges.

Now there is no choice. Although Hollis might be vindicated in a trial, he evidently cannot bear up under the rigors of open court hearings. The father takes steps to notify the police, prosecution and court of his son's condition and stipulate proceedings be carried out under Section 1370.1 PC. This law provides that because retarded persons cannot understand the nature of the charges against them, they be spared, and determination of the case be resolved after a study of the accused by a professional from a California State Regional Center for the Developmentally Disabled.

After the interrogation, Hollis' father locates a defense attorney with experience in cases involving the retarded. They work together on the case, sharing expertise and perceptions. Hollis' good fortune in having two such defenders is multiplied when a physically-handicapped judge is assigned to the case.

An evaluation is ordered by a local Regional Center which refers a qualified, experienced psychologist to make the study. This assignment is reviewed by the court on request of the defense attorney (who had written the Court's order for examination, since there was little precedent for the situation—Section 1370.1 was brand new then.)

After two reports by the consulting professional, the final evaluation holds that Hollis is indeed retarded, not a person of violent or antisocial inclinations, and best served by returning to his home.

This is not the end of the story—a female prosecuting attorney, whose attitudes paralleled those of the teacher in the fist illustration, decides that society's needs are best served by attempting to commit Hollis to an institution. She ignores the evaluation, sets her course of action without a determination of guilt or innocence, and attempts to impose her will.

Perhaps the prosecutor is trying to justify her public employment by blindly insisting that "protection of society" lies in commitment of Hollis. Fortunately, she fails.

Had the judge been a different person; had the defense attorney or Regional Center psychologist been a less-aware person; had Hollis been the son of a less-informed or motivated parent—the outcome might have been different.

But at least, in this illustration, the law allowed Hollis a chance for justice. Before the enactment of Section 1370.1 PC, there was no chance at all.

Justice Slips Her Blindfold

There are thousands of people, like Hollis or the person in our first illustration, who find themselves accused of a crime. It may be that the retarded person is more easily captured … or that the retarded person cannot defend himself or herself properly … or, as was partially the case of both these true stories, it may be that social bigotry toward someone who is *different* accounts for the situation.

Whatever the cause, thousands of citizens are today held in confinement against their will, without merit, merely because of their condition. Be it jail, prison, state hospitals, "community centered" facilities, or foster homes—involuntary commitment without humane concern for the rights of the retarded and/or developmentally disabled is cruel and unusual punishment.

The famed statue of Justice slips her blindfold under Section 1370.1 PC to take account of the variations in people, just as is done in other cases involving sanity.

We have long recognized the rights of the insane, both to be exempted from trial if the accused is incapable of understanding the nature of the charges or participating in his or her defense, and also in cases where the defendant is found to be of unsound mind during the commission of the alleged crime.

With the retarded or developmentally disabled, the law functions today in a different manner. To understand the difference between law affecting rights of the insane and law dealing with the retarded, it is first necessary to know the differences between the persons involved:

Normal: A person whose body and mind work pretty much like everyone else's. This is relative—a "normal" person in one context could be very different somewhere else.

Disabled: A person whose body or mind lacks some of the capabilities which are considered "normal," but who can compensate for this lack.

Retarded: A person whose mind from birth does not grow as much as the "normal" person's, who cannot, or only in a very limited way, compensate.

Mentally Ill: A "normal" person whose mind is affected by a sickness of one kind or another—usually curable.

These are not textbook definitions, only simplified guidelines to illustrate the differences between people.

These differences and their recognition by those who work professionally with the insane, retarded, and disabled led to a decision some years ago to attempt to rewrite California's penal code.

Leading attorneys, judges, law enforcement officials, doctors, and mental health professionals had been working on the problems raised by unclear provisions in the laws dealing with retarded and insane defendants.

At the same time, in California a movement was underway, led by parents of retarded persons, to establish community-based service facilities for care of the retarded and developmentally disabled. This movement led to the creation of the state's network of Regional Centers for the Developmentally Disabled, which now have 21 locations throughout the state.

Regional Centers augmented a haphazard system of state hospitals and privately-operated long term care facilities which previously had been the major locations for group care of the retarded and many developmentally disabled individuals. Some police officials took advantage of the creation of Regional Centers to informally divert obviously-retarded persons accused of a crime for interim attention while some effort would be made to resolve the problem before it reached the courtroom.

This was a risky procedure not sanctioned in law or police regulations. The alternative was to seek temporary commitment of the accused in a mental institution, which usually served neither defendant, police, nor society.

But then the options open to the court were limited also. Retarded defendants were often apparently sane. The law made no provisions for the impairments of judgment usually involved in retardation. The opinions of a professional mental health expert could only be couched in terms of sanity if the court was inclined to find some way under the law to recognize the accused's problems.

Until Section 1370.1 was enacted in late 1973, the law essentially said a retarded person accused of a crime faced only two options: Confinement in an institution until somehow a "cure" brought about ability of the accused to stand trial, or endure the ordeal of courtroom proceedings regardless of the accused's condition.

Now, under Section 1370.1 PC, the court is directed to consult with professionals who deal with the problems of the retarded to make two determinations before any effort is made to hold a trial: Is this defendant retarded? What disposition of this case best serves society and the individual needs of the accused—dismissal, return to home, confinement, or trial on the charges as brought?

There's room here for a wide range of options. There's no need for the kind of tragedy we saw in the first illustration, in which a person with a good home environment and loving family is suddenly forced into an institution at the taxpayers' expense and probable destruction of Peter as a functioning member of society.

However, we are a long way from seeing this revision in legal system reach effectiveness. Section 1370.1 PC is still largely unknown in our courtrooms and legal offices, psychiatric clinics, probation departments, and homes. The task of implementing the law must begin now … further delay is intolerable.

One of the first elements involved in setting this law to work is training of defense and prosecution attorneys in the functions of the law, and study by legal experts of the ways this new procedure alters courtroom relationships.

Training of attorneys involves far more than mere examination of pleadings and presentations. It must also involve thorough study of the problems of the retarded citizen, to develop an understanding of circumstances in the retarded person's life and surroundings. For attorneys on either side of a case to properly work with the court this level of understanding is a necessity.

Judges, too, must include proceedings under Section 1370.1 PC in their training programs. The California Judicial Council should be involved in this effort for both new judges and those now on the bench. Again, included in this program must be "sensitivity training" about the retarded.

Regional Centers need to develop outreach programs ranging from public information activities to contacts with police, attorneys and judges to spur implementation of Section 1370.1 PC. Special attention must be given by the Centers to the procedural steps to be used in making evaluations of retarded defendants—mere testing, for example, is insufficient to serve the needs of a retarded defendant in the evaluation process.

Joint effort by the public and Regional Centers to convince the state legislature and administration to provide adequate funding for this effort is equally vital. Health services, in general, are "easy" services to short fund, and legislators have been all too willing to make such cuts.

In the public at large, considerable time and effort is necessary to deal with bigotry and hostility toward the retarded. Far too many criminal complaints are lodged by hostile citizens solely because the target is a retarded person. This is a long-range need in implementing Section 1370.1 PC, since public opinion is an ever-present spectator in the courtroom.

With such efforts as outlined here to implement the law, the likelihood of the code being misused will be greatly diminished. Today, the law stands naked as a two-edged sword to be swung not only in defense of the retarded, but also at the retarded citizen. In its provisions are elements which could mean a life sentence of unneeded, unwanted custodial care, while misapplication of Section 1370.1 PC can also deprive a retarded person of important civil rights. Sensitive, informed legal specialists are less likely to allow for misuse of this law.

As both Presidents' Commissions noted, there are many, many problems confronting the law in dealing with the rights of the retarded or developmentally disabled. These problems are much broader than just civil rights in criminal matters. However, in context of Section 1370.1 PC, we need to consider these questions.

How does the court recognize that Section 1370.1 PC is applicable? How do this law's directives change the usual pattern of relationships between judges, attorneys, prosecutors, client, and other officers of the court? What is expected of the court? How does a court balance the grievances of the complainant and the rights of the accused? What are society's rights in this issue? Answers to some of these perplexing problems must be worked out in application of the law.

For now, let's make a couple of notes: First, far too little attention has been paid to this law. It is not the subject of seminars for judges and attorneys, little discussion is given to its structure in meetings of professionals who work with the retarded and or developmentally disabled, and virtually no one in the community at large is even aware of the problems of the retarded.

Second, when the public gets wind of the fact that "soft" judges can now stop a trial, hold a hearing and then "turn loose" a retarded defendant in the care of his parents in the community, all hell is likely to break out. But if the public is told of the humanity of retarded person, of emotions and feelings, if the public is taught about bigotry against the disabled—and then informed of the real intents and purposes of Section 1370.1 PC, perhaps reluctant officers of the court and Regional Center officials will feel freer to consider the rights of our retarded citizens. To quote Pete, in most cases involving the retarded, "Prison is not for me."

CHAPTER TWO

WHAT DOES THE LAW DO?

Numerous recent advances have been made in the redefinition of legal treatment of the insane and the retarded. The enactment of Section 1370.1 PC eliminates situations such as the decision rendered by the judge in the 1929 case of *People v. Phillips,* in which the remark was made, "The law doesn't attempt to measure intellect."

Some 30 years later, the court noted in *People v. Gorshen,* "In this state, there appears to be no statutory or judicial definition or test of idiocy or lunacy as related to the criminal state of mind."

That observation was a long step forward, but remained only as an observation until this law was enacted. Section 1370.1 PC itself lagged many years behind significant advances in the capability of professionals to test mental abilities and inclinations. Thanks largely to these advances, and the efforts by determined criminal defense lawyers to protect their client's rights, many possible injustices have been thwarted under normal criminal proceedings.

Even with Section 1370.1 in operation, there are other sections of the Penal code which bear archaic reference to "lunatics," "idiots," and other pejorative words which defy accurate definition in legal proceedings. It is up to the legislature in future sessions to purge the law of these vague, negative and unrealistic sections.

Speaking of the law, and its terms, let's look now at the exact words of Section 1370.1 PC:

CALIFORNIA PENAL CODE

1370.1   (Proceedings under Lanterman Mental Retardation Services Act of 1968, after court's order on finding defendant mentally retarded) Notwithstanding the provisions of Section 1370, if the court has reason to believe that the defendant's inability to understand the nature and purpose of the criminal proceedings taken against him so as to be able to conduct, or assist in, his own defense in a rational manner is a result of mental retardation, the trial or judgment shall be suspended, and the court shall order the regional center for the mentally retarded, which serves the counties in which the court is situated, and which is established under the Lanterman Developmental Disabilities Services Act, Division 25 (commencing with Section 38000) of the Health and Safety Code, to examine the defendant and within 90 days report to the court the results of the examination and its recommendation for the care and treatment of the defendant. The court may make such orders as may be necessary to provide for the examination of such person by the regional center and for the safekeeping, necessary medical treatment, care or restraint of the defendant pending further orders of the court following receipt of the regional center's report, in the county hospital, his own home, in a state hospital, or in such other place, excluding a jail, as will afford access to personnel of the regional center for the purpose of examination and suitable provisions for the safety and comfort of the defendant. If the regional center reports that the defendant is not mentally retarded, the court shall make the appropriate order under Section 1370. If the regional center reports that the defendant is mentally retarded and is a danger to himself or others and therefore subject to commitment to a state hospital pursuant to Article 5 (commencing with Section 6500), Chapter 2, Part 2, Division 6, of the Welfare and Institutions Code, the regional center shall recommend the initiation of proceedings to commit the defendant to a state hospital pursuant to Article 5. If the regional center reports that the defendant is mentally retarded but is not subject to commitment to a state hospital pursuant to Article 5, the regional center shall make such recommendations as it deems best for the care and treatment of the defendant. Upon receiving the report and recommendations of the regional center, the court shall order that commitment proceedings pursuant to Article 5 be instituted if such defendant is subject to commitment there under, or, if not so subject to commitment. It shall order the defendant placed in a home or facility, or state hospital recommended by the regional center for care and treatment or in some other home, facility, or state hospital approved by the regional center for the care and treatment of the defendant. The regional center shall reexamine each defendant placed in home or facility or state hospital, or committed to a state hospital, at least once each year to ascertain whether the mental retardation of the defendant has changed to such an extent that defendant is able to understand the nature and purpose of the criminal proceedings taken against him so as to be able to conduct, or assist in, his own defense in a rational manner. If the regional center ascertains that the mental retardation of the defendant has changed to such an extent, it shall certify the finding to the sheriff and district attorney of the county, and the court wherein the defendant's case is pending. The sheriff shall thereupon, without delay, bring the defendant from the home, facility, or state hospital, as the case may be, and place him in proper custody until he is brought to trail or judgment, as the case may be, or is legally discharged. In event of dismissal of the criminal charges before such certification is made, the person shall be rereferred to the appropriate regional center for services under the Lanterman Developmental Disabilities Services Act, Division 25 (commencing with Section 38000) of the Health and Safety Code.

Those long sentences and references can get to be a mouthful. But rather than devote the following pages to a dessicated dissection of the legalese, let's go through the procedures the law provides for.

The moment a retarded person comes before the court, not at the police station or anywhere else, but at the moment he or she is to report to the courtroom for the first procedure involving a judge, Section 1370.1 PC gets involved.

This is the first place, <u>in</u> <u>the</u> <u>present</u> <u>terms</u> <u>of</u> <u>the</u> <u>law,</u> where an informed, astute person who knows the problems of the retarded is needed. When the accused has friends or family to stand up in court, we have some assurance the law can be met...if friends, family or court know about Section 1370.1 PC. But this is the first test of the court's awareness of this law and its operations.

The moment retardation is recognized, the prosecutor should be notified, and the judge should be informed. Subsequently, prosecution and defense should make a motion that this matter be referred to a Regional Center.

Checkpoint number two: Framing the motion for examination. The court's charge to the center later determines what kind of language the examiner's report includes. This requires informed, capable attorneys and judge, also.

At this point, the defendant is realistically in the custody of the Regional Center, under supervision of the court. A professional person is to be assigned by the Center to make an evaluation of the defendant and give a recommendation to the court. This defendant is retarded and needs special attention of some kind. This defendant is not retarded and should continue through trial.

Here the defense attorney earns his fee. The defense attorney must stand up for the interests of the client, first by insisting that a truly qualified psychiatrist, psychologist, therapist or case worker be assigned to the case.

Next, the attorney's job is to seek a recommendation to the court that clearly is in his or her client's best interests. This requires an understanding of what the professional is going to look for, testing methods, variations in interpretations, possible bias about retarded persons, and so forth. A capable attorney will be able to help the professional write a report that the court can accept. A capable defense attorney can work with the evaluator and the prosecuting attorney to reach a final report acceptable to all parties.

Checkpoint number three: Does the defense attorney have experience with the problems of the retarded? Can the attorney effectively deal with Regional Center staffs and employees?

Every defence attorney will accord his or her developmentally disabled client with the same professional respect due all other clients. The fact of the client's disability should not produce an attitude of arrogance, insolence or undue feelings of superiority towards the client. It is the duty of the defense attorney to press for a dismissal. Oddly enough, there are many defense attorneys who don't recognize this as one of their jobs.

The Regional Center worker has a period of time in which to make the evaluation. Today's skills in this area are quite high—testing, interviews, and many other techniques very clearly give a qualified professional an understanding of the person's capabilities.

At the end of the evaluation, the most important part of the report is the paragraph or two that recommends disposition of the accused. Unless the court has other reasons to guide its decision, usually this recommendation will be followed.

Checkpoint number four: How does the Regional Center worker view the assignment. Look out! If in this sudden new role the assigned professional sees himself or herself as protector of society, as judge, jury and prosecutor all at once, then the accused client is in danger. The Regional Center evaluator is not assigned to determine even the potential of the accused to commit whatever act is alleged in the criminal complaint. The evaluator is assigned to look at the mental and intellectual state of the accused, and determine what form of attention is best for that person.

More than misconduct by police, attorneys or judges, the Regional Center staff person who takes a negative posture going in toward the retarded or disabled defendant is a menace to all retarded citizens.

Once the report is in, it is up to the court to make a determination in the case. The law strictly provides that if the defendant is found to be retarded, provisions be made for the care and safety of the accused, and all other proceedings are stopped.

Here is where we encounter several of the problems with this law. First of all, as we saw in the story of Hollis, if there are malicious or false accusations levied against a retarded citizen, recourse to civil action is barred. After all, in this case the charges against the accused go into limbo. The case, unless the court also make a dismissal, remains unresolved in the files.

Next, the law now reads that as long as the case remains unresolved the accused must submit to annual reevaluations by the Regional Center. Now, in the case of retarded or developmentally disabled person, there is no cure for the condition. It is indeed a lifelong condition. The law, however, treats this problem the same as mental illness: Once the defect is cured the accused must stand trial.

If the court resolves to commit the accused to an institution, the decision is generally a permanent commitment. It is important for the court to recognize that institutions are not necessarily the proper place. This question must be raised because some judges may be inclined to select institutionalization as a compromise between the wishes of the defense and the complaints of the prosecution and victim.

Finally, there is uncertainty about the appeals process following a case of this nature. This is a question that needs much more examination, and probably won't be dealt with until after the fact—or, once a decision is reached that the defense says is unfair.

All of the preceding paragraphs about the function of Section 1370.1 PC assume that somehow the retarded defendant is known to be retarded when he or she first goes to court.

But there is no experience yet with courts interrupting normal proceedings to determine the condition of the accused. And what should a probation officer do when suddenly it is determined a recently-convicted person is retarded?

This kind of question is in the same class as the question of proper behavior by the police when they first develop contact with a retarded person. Police have no discretionary power in these cases: Either take the person to the station, or if the person appears to be violently mentally ill or retarded, take him or her to a medical facility for 72-hours' detention.

If a psychiatrist on the facility's staff thinks it necessary, that detention can be stretched to 10 days. If there is medical opinion that longer detention is necessary, it becomes pretty sticky trying to get a person out of one of these institutions.

This is another well-known horror story we only need mention. State mental facilities are usually overpopulated and understaffed. In many cases, patients are drugged, for the convenience of the staff, not because they are of any particular danger.

The structure of Section 1370.1 PC, and its shortcomings, bring us to one important question: Is it possible to guarantee a retarded person Constitutional rights of a fair trial, and still keep that person out of the trauma of the judicial process?

This same question is raised by the President's Commission, which stated.

"The significant question is whether it is possible to enjoy the benefits of both alternatives. Can there be an increase in the sensitivity of the judicial system to retardation without risking a real deterioration of the retarded offender's role as victim of the system.

"The sense of victimization of retarded persons generally seems to be at stake. If these citizens are subject as a group to deprivations, discrimination and hostility whenever they come to the consciousness of the community, there is almost everything to lose and nothing to gain by focusing on retardation as an aspect of the criminal justice system.

"If, on the other hand, the dominant theme of the mentally retardeds' relations with society is one of benevolent concern and active care, a program to sensitize the criminal justice system makes a good deal of sense."

First and last checkpoint: The value of laws such as Section 1370.1 PC hinges entirely on the attitudes of the persons in the judicial system ... and on the willingness of the community at large to accept this law as a useful approach to jurisprudence.

Peter's story is a case history of the opportunities for application of Section 1370.1 PC—and for its misuse. Had the court been able to divert Peter to a Regional Center for an evaluation, the boy's parents might have been able to prevent his institutionalization. The defense attorney might have been able to argue, effectively, that the pressure of an uninvolved third party was outright bigotry, and society's needs were ill-served by the removal of Peter from his home. But under the law as it stood then, such an argument was irrelevant to the case.

Even so, a sensitive judge could well have known Peter did not need to be dragged from his home. It could have been the court chose the resolution it did as an alternative to branding the youth as a sex offender and causing him to register with the police, if a charitable view is conjectured.

The prosecutor could easily have pressed for dismissal of the case had the provisions of Section 1370.1 PC been available.

Ultimately, the woman who thought it her duty to put Peter away might never have taken such a measure had the long-range approach to implementing Section 1370.1 PC been underway ... the public information effort.

For Peter, though, it is too late. For his retarded brethren, there's still a chance.

CHAPTER THREE
DRAMATIS PERSONAE

Role playing in lives of persons dealing with Section 1370.1 PC can, and should be, rehearsed. A missed entrance in this drama can have far more serious consequences than a flub during a play.

But, to continue for a moment our parallel, an informed cast can make up for the missing character, just as must be done in the theater—and, unlike the stage, the script can be rewritten later when one of the players discovers that Section 1370.1 PC has an unrecognized role.

In the following pages, a capsule outline details, the interrelated functions of everyone affected by this law. It is an overview needed by all, so that each person cab be more effective in serving the intent of the law as well as the needs of the accused and society.

Parents: nothing is more horrifying, for any parent, than to receive the word that police have taken their child into custody.

Immediately, tell the authorities the child is retarded or developmentally disabled. Next, call the law enforcement agency's attention to Section 1370.1 PC. If the agency is unfamiliar with the law, ask them to contact the local Regional Center, or offer to pay for the cost of a call to the California Association for the Retarded in Sacramento, or refer to this book, so the police understand what occurs in cases involving the retarded.

Under normal circumstances, police procedure calls for investigation of the complaint, and questioning of those making the complaint, entry of a report, and a search for suspects. In the event of a crime in process or a violent crime in which there is an urgent need to apprehend a suspect, every effort is made to locate potential perpetrators and if there is enough evidence, or unresolved suspicions on the part of the enforcement agency pointing to a particular suspect, an arrest is made.

In complaints where time permits probing, police agencies usually attempt to gather enough information to warrant a judgment about the potential courtroom durability of the charge. Although it happens on rare occasions, capricious complains are not usually accepted by the police.

Eventually, the file is presented to the city attorney or district attorney for examination. At this point a judgment is made whether or not to continue the case. In this situation, an informed parent or defense attorney might be able to confer with the police and prosecutor's office to have the case concluded before it goes any further.

At this point, as well as in later stages of a case under Section 1370.1 PC, it is necessary to make one major evaluation: Capability of the accused to commit such an act, and, capability of the accused to participate in, and understand, court proceedings.

In these cases, as in all events involving criminal allegations, the balance point between Society's interests and those of each defendant is the capacity of the accused.

Objectivity, per se, is not the question—Section 1370.1 PC patently precludes objectivity by offering humane exclusions from the penal codes. Be prepared for an effort by the police and prosecution to go forward with a case if in their opinion the defendant, though retarded, is capable of the accusation.

If that qualification is made, if the accused does meet those standards, and if the accusation itself is not of the nearly-frivolous type noted in our opening illustrations, then it may be in the best interests of all parties to proceed through court actions. Among other things, vindication if received is far more beneficial to the accused than the unresolved limbo which deprives the defendant of other civil rights.

Take away this qualification, however, and under no circumstances is any criminal proceeding justified. This is a new category—the accused is not insane, but also lacks the prerequisites for commiting most crimes. (Again, that person who is a danger to himself and society receives very specific attention under the points of the law.)

From this point forward, the case lies in the hands of others. The parent, guardian or friend of the retarded accused should know and watch the actions of prosecutor, defense attorney, police and judge to guard against any diversion of the proper course of the case.

One final note, here, about Regional Centers: After a two-year battle, with Regional Center directors led by Dennis Amundson, the author succeeded in having centers listed in the white and yellow pages of the phone book. Hopefully when you need to get in touch with a Center—you can now use the phone book.

Law Enforcement Agencies: in general, the law and departmental regulations specifically describe the latitude officers have in probing a crime, making reports, and dealing with suspects.

Police regulations are usually too strict in dictating the handcuffing and disposition of a "prisoner" when that person is retarded. There is usually no need, for example, to cuff a docile, retarded suspect who may not yet be accused of the crime involved—and the effect of placing such a prisoner into handcuffs is horrendously negative.

The most important aspect of police work in cases involving a retarded citizen is the initial questioning of the complainant: If this were a "normal" person, would this complaint be pursued? Is this devotion of police time and effort producing a needed protection of society, or merely satisfying the bigotry of a fearful citizen toward the accused?

Decidedly, the second most important element of the law enforcement agency's activity is the "Observations and Conclusions" section of the investigating officer's report: Mention that the suspect is apparently retarded and the case should come under the clauses of Section 1370.1 PC.

Ultimately, it would be to the general community's benefit if several officers and supervisory persons were given special sensitivity training to improve their capacities to recognize the problems of the retarded, and case law involving the retarded.

Prosecution: Cases involving retarded citizens seem to have a special niche in most city attorneys' and district attorneys' offices. Some kind of "sensitivity" tells prosecutors that charges against retarded citizens are more grave than when "normal" people are involved.

Prosecutors, in general, take such cases much more seriously. Whereas the case against a "normal" person might be declined as near-frivolous, when a retarded citizen is involved, there's an extra measure of seriousness.

So, the first thing prosecuting attorneys need to consider is whether complaints against the retarded really justify expenditure of the taxpayer's money.

Naturally, in those instances where the prosecutor looks at the case and rejects it because a retarded person is involved, there is every reason to support such decisions. But in other cases, those which result in the kind of tragedy which opened this book, the first question the attorney should ask is, "Would this be a worthwhile case against anyone but a retarded citizen?"

Prosecutors have many options which are not open to either the police, court, or defense. A prosecutor sets the tone against which the case is judged. A prosecutor can argue for, and obtain, a dismissal in most cases. A prosecutor can recognize the humane considerations in dealing with cases which require the court's attention, but obviously do not demand incarceration or institutionalization. Should plea-bargaining, or some compromise by the court, become a necessity, the level of the prosecution's demands define the range in which final disposition is set.

Section 1370.1 PC really enters the picture when the police or sheriff's report is filed with the prosecutor's office. Assuming it is known the defendant is retarded, the prosecutor takes a different approach, and in that context should not only examine the merits of the case, but also attempt to forecast the outcome of the process once a judge and professional evaluator become a part of the action.

In the event it is not noted a defendant is retarded, if the prosecution has reason to contact the defendant or any friends or relatives prior to the first court date, the city attorney or district attorney should include in observations an attempt to determine the status of the accused. *It is a statutory obligation of the prosecution to tell the court a defendant comes under the terms of Section 1370.1 PC.*

There are many occasions when the prosecution must choose between attempting to carry a case to its ultimate conclusion or accepting either a dismissal or other resolution recommended by the Regional Center evaluator. In cases involving a retarded defendant, the traditional adversary relationship is inappropriate unless and until the court decides to proceed with a criminal action.

Yes, it is proper and necessary to cast a critical eye upon motions and recommendations, to insure a wholly-correct course of action by the court. No, it is not proper to adamantly oppose all actions taken or suggested on behalf of the accused merely because the prosecution is the prosecution. The taxpayers support prosecutors to seek justice, not necessarily a long record of convictions for the sake of the record.

It is always appropriate for the prosecution, when a defendant is recognized as retarded, to interrupt court proceedings to suggest that Section 1370.1 PC should be used. Since some defendants will not be initially recognized as retarded, or this section of law will be made known to the prosecution during a proceeding against a retarded person, after action is underway, there should be no concern that introducing this element constitutes an embarrassment or an improper action by the prosecution.

In cases under Section 1370.1 PC, the defense attorney and prosecution are partners working to protect the needs of society and of the defendant. Both attorneys should work together to find a resolution—not, as in other cases, to produce a resolution that synthesizes their opposing positions.

Most prosecution offices will more effectively meet the demand if a special section is set aside to deal with charges against retarded citizens. As in the case with law enforcement agencies, attorneys assigned to these units should take pains to become aware of the needs and capabilities of the retarded.

California's legislators, so willing to make this law available, should take the next logical step and provide—mandate, even—for training programs at Regional Center to develop this capacity among all prosecuting offices in the state's cities and counties.

Defense attorneys: Both defense attorneys and public defenders today are generally unaware of Section 1370.1 PC—and, in the offices of public defenders, considerations of clauses such as this law are often only minor considerations. The use of this law should be a primary consideration.

It is the defense role to fight for the rights of the accused. Therefore, in these cases, it becomes a matter of major significance that the defending attorney be experienced in use of Section 1370.1 PC, that orders for evaluation be familiar to the lawyer, and that the defending attorney have intimate knowledge of the problems of retardation. It could be a basis for legal malpractice to take a case with less knowledge.

On first taking a case involving a retarded citizen who is being held in custody, inquire about a conservatorship- find out if anyone holds a conservatorship of the accused. Presentation of conservatorship papers can be useful in obtaining release of the accused on his or her own recognizance in custody of the conservator.

If possible, intervene with the prosecution when the enforcement agency turns over the case for review by the prosecution. Depending upon the merits of the case, it may be possible to prevent filing of charges.

However, once a case is in court, it is imperative that all proceedings be halted until the Regional Center in the area has been ordered to make an evaluation. Phrasing of the order makes a major difference in what will be reported back to the court. Not only does the order determine what level of professional will be assigned to the case, but also whether the professional merely tests the defendant or goes further.

If the Regional Center delays assignment; if the person assigned is unqualified; if the evaluator is desultory, "objective," or hostile; if the evaluator refuses to provide interim reports to the defense, then the court must be petitioned for a hearing on reassignment of the evaluator.

The defense must stay on top of the case at all times. This is unlike many other kinds of cases which after basic trial preparations can be set aside until the court date—the defense needs to monitor the accused's circumstances, progress of the evaluation, and drafting of the final report.

It may be necessary to bring in another, independent evaluator if the person assigned to the case is patently uninterested in the needs or problems of the accused.

Special attention, too, needs to be paid to the relatives of the accused. Concerned kin can be very useful in the defense of the accused. However, the defense attorney should be prepared for those who find their relative's disability an embarrassment, who wish only to be relieved of the burden of care. In that situation the defense may be forced to speak on behalf of the defendant in opposition to the wishes of family as well as to the attempts of the prosecution.

Regional Centers: Establishment of Regional Centers for the Developmentally Disabled in California was the first step taken to provide an official advocate on behalf of the retarded and developmentally disabled. Although these agencies, as a result of political bickering, public inattention and underfunding, have not conducted the type of outreach campaign necessary to influence the community at large in matters affecting the retarded, the very existence of Regional Centers is an immeasurable boon to an abused, neglected minority.

In the very nature of the Regional Center, then, is the direction that should be taken when a retarded citizen is evaluated in a criminal proceeding. *The Regional Center is first an advocate for the retarded person. The professional assigned to the task is not there merely to test, or to provide therapy, or to be "objective:" The task is to determine capability of the client to have even committed the deed he or she is accused of, and the capability of that person to understand the court's subsequent actions. If it is clear the retarded client cannot meet these criteria, the Center must recommend to the court what disposition is best for the client.*

"Best for the client" is a far cry from "what will satisfy the prosecution." It is also a far cry from a cynical effort to make a lifetime dependant of a retarded person, either in "therapy" when unneeded, or in placing the client into a foster home, hospital, or other institution when unnecessary.

Foremost obligation of the Center is to provide individual, rather than formula, treatment of the client. Section 1370.1 PC makes individual exceptions of retarded defendants accused of a crime; the same client deserves parallel attention from the Regional Center.

Given the range of other duties Regional Centers must fill, it is necessary to have on staff or as "vendors" a pool of qualified professionals familiar with Section 1370.1 PC evaluations. This may require training programs, which should be run by experienced attorneys as well as experienced professionals, and may require an attorney on staff or available to consult with the evaluators.

Professional evaluator: Much as an attorney must employ every basic Constitutional argument in defense of the accused, so the mental health professional making the evaluation must employ every available means to develop a profile of the client. This includes not only such standard techniques as psychometric testing for brain damage, but also psychological evaluation; analysis of the client'' home environment; thorough comparison of the criminal charges, plus all investigative reports, with the accused's capacities; and the other qualifying factors that should influence the court's final disposition.

The criminal complaint has no bearing on the evaluation, except in terms of the capacity of the accused to commit the crime. The severity of the charge should make no difference in terms of recommending final disposition.

The court wants to know the intellectual abilities of the accused as well as the defendant's emotional condition. All recommendations should be couched in these terms. Usually the court will direct the Regional Center to submit a report within a certain time span; interim reports may be also requested.

Probation officer: It should become increasingly unusual for a probation officer to be asked for a report on a convicted defendant who is retarded. However, when and if a defendant is found during a probation study to be retarded, or if the officer making the study has reason to suspect the defendant is retarded, the court, defense attorney, and prosecution should all be notified the defendant may deserve benefit of Section 1370.1 PC. The probation report should be suspended until the court has held a hearing on the matter and given direction to the probation officer.

In this circumstance, it is probable the defendant has neither family nor friends to speak on his or her behalf. The family may be reluctant to assist the defendant—an automatic clue that something is wrong. When a case involving a retarded person reaches this stage, the probation officer is for all practical purposes the last friend of the defendant.

Judge: It is not ever necessary to do anything more in open court than order an evaluation from a Regional Center and subsequently make orders for final disposition of a defendant in a case involving Section 1370.1 PC. Given cooperative attitudes by the prosecution and defense counsels, all other activities can take the place of customary plea bargaining sessions.

Assuming the case goes to arraignment, two questions must be resolved—preparation of an order for evaluation, and custody of the accused both prior to and during evaluation. Section 1370.1 PC stipulates the accused must be available to the Regional Center, and in a location other then a jail.

The order for evaluation must direct the Regional Center to meet standards necessary for the court to make an informed decision. So, if the order is too vague, the report may be insufficient. If the order is overly specific, useful information may be excluded from the report. Consulting both counsel in the case and precedent orders, such as that which is in exhibit in this book, is a reasonable course.

Housing the accused while the order is in preparation, and during evaluation, is a more difficult question. It involves an immediate, superficial evaluation—should the defendant be released to the custody of family, placed in a foster residence, or in some other facility? Should bond be posted? Whatever the decision, it must also reflect the intent of Section 1370.1 PC to prevent unnecessary disruption or disturbance of the defendant.

In setting a time period over which the evaluation of the defendant is to be conducted, the court is wise to allow enough time for a preliminary study to be issued. This provides guidance for defense and prosecution to begin efforts at reaching an acceptable resolution in consultation with the court and the evaluator.

The court's greatest dilemma may lie in attempting to provide for fair disposition of the accused while leaving a case unresolved. The terms of Section 1370.1 PC clearly allow for dismissal of charges in cases where the retarded defendant is incapable of participating in further proceedings.

In all the preceding paragraphs, every effort has been made to deal with all parties to a case involving a retarded accused. One important party has been left out: The accuser.

Choice of this word over that of "victim" is deliberate. Repeatedly the difference between capacity and incapacity has been stressed as a social requirement, a standard of judgment. To that person who enters the complaint, the standard of judgment is a sense of being wronged.

However, a "victim" is someone who wrongly, improperly, and undeservedly suffers a loss of some kind. An "accuser" is a person who makes such a charge so that others not involved in the event may return with a judgment based on the facts. The fact of retardation is inescapable. In many, perhaps most, criminal complaints it eliminates the concept of criminality.

It is no injustice to acknowledge that no criminality exists in an action which the accuser asserts, even correctly, occurred. To find otherwise, where the facts warrant humans considerations, is to make the retarded defendant the victim. In such a case, there is no justice, only two victims.

Some people are by situation or personal habit unable to be as noble as this implies. This is why society, in Section 1370.1 PC, assumes the mantle of nobility.

CHAPTER FOUR

SPECIAL ATTENTION TO THE EVALUATOR AND DEFENSE COUNSEL

From the retarded accused's point of view, two extremely important figures are the defense attorney and the mental health professional who is assigned to evaluate him or her for the court.

Extra attention must be paid to both these parties by those who take up the cause of the retarded defendant. Attorneys and psychologists or psychiatrists who wish to become more active in these fields deserve more information than simple guidelines about their activities in court.

Depending upon the Regional Center to which the case is referred, the parents and/or defense counsel may have some role in selecting the person who will make the evaluation. It is possible, although difficult, to challenge the assignment made. Whatever the case, before the retarded accused is subjected to even the first meeting, advocates for the defendant must make a judgment about the evaluator.

First, probe the evaluator's competence. This is accomplished both by documenting that person's professional credentials (and checking them out), as well as by asking proving questions of the professional's experience and attitudes.

If the professional is satisfactory, it is then only necessary to follow the steps outlined previously. However, if the appointment is unsatisfactory, the first step should be a meeting with the Regional Center's executive director to seek reassignment.

In the event that session is unproductive, the next step is to contact the state administrative officers for Regional Centers—the name, address, and phone number of the person in charge is in the California State Roster, available at your community library. Lacking that contact, go to the state director of health.

Other resources for the dissatisfied advocate include the California Association of the Retarded, in Sacramento, or the local Citizens Advocate program. This latter program, something like a "Big Brother" program for the retarded citizen, is rapidly becoming a statewide organization—a chapter in any community will be listed in the telephone book.

In the absence of satisfaction, as noted before, the defense should bring in its own expert to present a counter-proposal to the court. This soon becomes very messy, since the court will then be called upon to decide which expert is more expert in problems affecting the retarded. It is a last-resort measure.

Psychologists and psychiatrists who wish to become active in this field should become recognized "vendors" with Regional Centers. By doing so, the mental health professional becomes an accredited consultant to the agency, on call for services such as evaluations. To become a vendor, there is a specified sequence of steps and standards to meet, including approval by the Regional Center's executive director.

Selecting a defense attorney is both a more difficult and simple task for the friends or kin of the accused.

Again, it may be useful to contact friends, Regional Center staffs, or the California Association for the Retarded for recommendations. The attorney selected should definitely have had experience with other retarded clients; should have had experience in cases involving Section 1370.1 PC; and should be familiar with the problems of the retarded.

It is not sufficient for a defense attorney to tell the prospective client's representatives, "Oh, that isn't necessary—all we have to know is the law." Sensitivity and insight are paramount in these cases.

Unfortunately, most Regional Centers neither recognize requirement nor have the budget to pay the fees for defense of retarded citizens in Section 1370.1 PC cases. This should be a Regional Center function through its vendor program. Attorneys are urged to press for this.

As a result, these cases will usually be either "pro bono," for the public good, or they will be regular fee cases.

No attorney should rebuff or resent probing by the family. If any potential defense attorney is in any sense arrogant or insensitive to the concerns of the defendant's advocates, that's an attorney who should not be selected. Conversely, anxious friends or relatives should not become an unnecessary burden to the competent, experienced legal advocate.

By advising the public to go to attorneys with experience in these cases, it might seem the process is self-eliminating for lawyers: How otherwise does an attorney gain the experience?

The first, and most obvious answer, is to provide a proper legal specialization program for representation of the retarded—not only in criminal matters, but in such other civil areas as probate, estate planning, conservatorships, etc.

Beyond that, it is proper for attorneys to work with Regional Centers in the myriad matters which demand legal expertise. Attorneys should also become visibly active in community affairs involving the retarded, and should press their various associations for programs, such as seminars dealing with the problems of the retarded in the law and society.

Much has been made of the attorney who is interested in having access to the estates and financial affairs of the retarded, at the expense of the client. Any citizen aware of such abuses must make complaints to the local Bar Association to put an end to such practices. Ultimately, however, it is the profession's responsibility to provide greater access by all lawyers to service to the retarded—this is only accomplished by encouragement through attention to the issues.

CHAPTER FIVE

THE PLACE OF THE DEVELOPMENTALLY DISABLED IN SOCIETY

Today, thanks to long struggle and concern by a few dedicated persons, the retarded person is slowly climbing up from the bottom of the social trash pile. That was the place, according to general society, for the developmentally disabled.

The retarded citizen deserves a position of freedom in this society, first, merely on the basis of guaranteed rights to life, liberty and the pursuit of happiness. The developmentally disabled citizen by general nature is a more orderly, less-aggressive person than the "normal" citizen.

It is long past the time for society to confront its own values, its deep-rooted bigotry and false perceptions of the retarded citizen. For successful operation of laws such as

Section 1370.1 PC, it is a necessity … but this is even more a necessity in our dream of a just and humane society.

To raise a community that is as humane as possible, we must see and know the many aspects of mankind. Physical aspects are apparent … living styles, although many avoid seeing these variations, are yet before us daily. We are now confronting the problems of the mentally ill in more open fashion than ever before.

Nobody has really found a way to cope with the problems of the mentally disabled person. Society only partially attempts to meet this problem, perhaps largely because our social structure does not include a principle of community responsibility for such persons as the retarded.

There's a special distinction here — we do recognize the social obligations to the developmentally disabled … but the community at large excludes the retarded from its awareness.

We try to provide sheltered workshops or other types of employment for the retarded person. We try to provide some sort of minimally sheltered life. For example, some agencies are experimenting with buying condominia for retarded residents. Part of that experiment is an effort to gauge the reaction to the program: Will the retarded resident then be subjected to official harrassment; zoning restrictions; neighborhood persecutions. This two-level effort on the one hand tries to make it possible for a retarded citizen to live in a normal, albeit slightly sheltered manner, in the community at large, but then acknowledges the bigotry that results when the neighbors find out.

When other minorities began agitating for protection of their rights, it was said that "You can't legislate attitudes." That is just what was done, and the result today is great forward movement from the status of affairs in the mid-1960's.

We can thank the physically handicapped for showing it is possible to achieve progress in legislating the rights of the retarded. Even though building inspectors go along with reluctant builders who don't want to change their designs to accommodate the handicapped, there are many other communities exerting great effort to enforce the new laws.

That advance was not scored without consistent, militant efforts by advocates for the handicapped going from place to place making the point. Those who wish to enlist in the struggle for the rights of the retarded are equally faced with a need to organize and fight.

There's a tremendous barrier in the way. Most people regard the retarded at least as curiosities, if not outright repulsive. Even in the mildest forms of disability, those who do not understand are usually frightened of the "different" person.

It's a universal truism that people, including our disabled, desire to be accepted. For example, at a meeting of artists and writers in Los Angeles, a woman with an artificial limb was to be the speaker. She had come from New York to make the presentation, but before she could go into the meeting, she still needed several drinks. She was asked why she had to "load up" before the session, and answered, "I've got to appear normal, and I don't feel that way unless I have a few drinks first."

We want to belong, to be admired, to be spoken with, to have other people interested in us. Retarded people are no different, except that they know they look, act, talk, and in some manner appear different and will never be completely accepted.

From birth, the retarded person knows his. The behavior of others around them, the hostility of strangers ... those attitudes are a terrible reality for the retarded.

To defend the rights of the disabled, it may be necessary to be aggressive, to answer hostility with hostility, rudeness with rudeness. This is hardly the "Love your neighbor" ethic … it is rather a confrontation ethic designed to shock the ignorant or bigoted person. So many layers of sugar-coated kindness toward "those people" insulate the average citizens from the reality of his or her true attitudes toward the disabled that it seems to require a shock to peel away the hypocrisy, recognized or not.

Far too many of our institutions, as has been alleged throughout this text, are filled with persons who don't care about the retarded. The policemen who think "retards" or "dummies" ought to be kept off the streets … the prosecutor who feels his or her job is justified only when another victim of the system is put away in a hospital … the Regional Center director or therapist who really doesn't find any value in trying to rehabilitate someone whose condition is permanent, and so does only testing to insure the commitment of the victim … the judge who knows what's best for society, even if the other parties involved don't. …

Regional Centers, for one, have become much too autonomous. Regional Centers should be purged of staff workers who don't care about the retarded. The Centers should be monitored by parents and advocates for the retarded, since that's where the courts go for advice and information.

If there's a potential weak spot in the entire sequence of implementing Secton 1370.1 PC, it is the Regional Center. At all other levels of the process, there's a form of checks and balances — defense and prosecution attorneys, law enforcement and courts, appeals judges and trial judges ... but the Regional Center professional assigned to this case is the linchpin of the whole proceeding.

About the only way to deal with this effectively is to devote tremendous professional attention to the role of mental health professionals in court proceedings. This has been done, extensively, in areas involving insanity — now it must be done for the benefit of our retarded citizens.

The profession must qualify specialists to work with courts in making evaluations, and make these specialists available throughout the Regional Center system. The profession must expose and eliminate any system of favoritism by Regional Centers, when and where it may exist, in accepting consultants to work on these cases.

Review and selection panels should be developed to monitor the work of these professionals, so that some form of appeal of the professional evaluation might be made before an innocent person is victimized by unprofessional conduct.

Trust, ultimately, is what will make this system function properly. When we can be satisfied as citizens that our social structure is making its best efforts to deal humanely with the retarded, we can be trusting. Some skepticism must always remain, lest our efforts be frustrated. However, we must struggle to reach the day when we can be trustful.

First of all, without this trust, our retarded citizens themselves will be uneasy. Even more than those "normal" persons in this world, the retarded person depends on trust and honesty for survival.

Second, those of us who are friends, relatives and parents of the retarded will never know happiness if our kin are surrounded by the slavering wolves who today employ deceit, bigotry and hatred on this defenseless minority. Ultimately, the retarded person must stand alone in the community, without family to care or friends to help … unless the community at large takes the retarded to its heart with concern and respect.

It was concern, respect, and love which led to the establishment of Section 1370.1 PC. And those principles must now guide us in insuring its productive application.

Exhibit #1 — Court Order for Evaluation

Attorney for Defendant

IN THE MUNICIPAL COURT OF __________________

JUDICIAL DISTRICT

COUNTY OF _______________________________ ,

STATE OF CALIFORNIA

THE PEOPLE OF THE STATE OF CALIFORNIA Plaintiff, vs. Defendant.	CASE NO. ORDER PURSUANT TO 1370.1 P.C.

Defendant having appeared by counsel, _______________

and the Court having reason to believe that the defendant is

unable to understand the nature and purpose of criminal

proceedings taken against him so as to be able to conduct

or assist in, his own defense in a rational manner as a result

of mental retardation, it is ordered that criminal

proceedings be suspended, and the defendant report

forthwith to Dr. ______X_____, licensed Psychologist

vendored by the Regional Centers for the Developmentally Disabled. Dr. ___X___ is ordered to examine the defendant and prepare a report for the Court and make recommendations as to the safe keeping, necessary medical treatment, care or restraint of the defendant. Said report is to be submitted on or before set date. Defendant is ordered to return to Division 00 in the courthouse located at blank street, city on set date at 8:30 A.M.

DATED:

____

, Judge

Signature

Exhibit #2 – Evaluator's report to Defense Attorney

Dear Defense Attorney:

Persuant to your request re: your client, I am writing to inform you that I am a clinical psychologist, licensed by the California Board of Medical Examiners, and am also registered by the Regional Centers for the Developmentally Disabled.

I have been seeing your client since the beginning of a month on a weekly basis for guidance and counseling. It is my considered opinion that the work I am doing with __X__ is consistent with the provisions of Penal Code Section 1370.1 and should be helpful to you and the court in assessing _____X_____ situation.

_______X_____ is a pleasant, cooperative young man who functions in the mildly mentally retarded range. He has always had special schooling for his handicap. In reviewing his past history and records from private school, special classes in the public school (emr), and hospital records, it is clear that he was born handicapped.

_______X_______ has been fortunate to have had some excellent educational programs. Even so, he is functioning at about a third grade level academically, and is noted to be both socially and emotionally immature. He shows no signs of aggressive behaviors now or in his past records. He presently seems quite confused as to what is going on in relation to his being picked up and questioned by the police.

Furthermore, _____X_____ has a moderate to severe speech and articulation problem which may easily be misunderstood by the general public. In the past his poor language facility and articulation problems have resulted in his being made fun of by some. In such situations,_____X_ tends to become quiet and/or leave the situation.

I trust this information will prove helpful to you and the court.

Yours Sincerely,

Signature

Exhibit #3 – Evaluator's report to Court

The Honorable Judge

Municipal Court

Division 00

_______________________ Any street

_______________________ California Municipality, 90000

Dear Sir,

In response to your order to examine (Defendant), Case No. __________, and to assist the court in making a determination on him, I am forwarding the following report.

From March 4, 1976 to June 12, 1976, I saw ___X___ weekly. Since June 12th, I am having bi-monthly sessions with him. During this time, I have performed psychological examination of ___X___, visited and had conferences with his teachers, counselor, school nurse, private speech therapist, and have had several sessions with his parents.

I have obtained all past reports available, going back to when ______X______ was 22 months old and was seen at ________ the Hospital on an ongoing basis for medical and psychological assistance. A copy of his cumulative record from City Schools, covering the time from elementary through high school and including his health, psychological, and educational reports has also been obtained.

Based on all of the above, it is my considered opinion that ______X______ was born handicapped and has neurological problems which reflect themselves in a moderate to severe speech and articulation difficulty. He functions within the mildly mentally retarded range, and has been in special classes through his school years.

______X______ is a likeable, cooperative young man who tries hard to please and has a pleasant manner. Those individuals who have known ______X______ over an extended period, describe him as a young man who avoids fights, bickering and confrontations, and who is eager to please.

During his period of therapy with me, I have not found any indications that would lead me to suspect aggressive behavior now, or in his past conduct. He is socially and emotionally immature. Academically, he functions at about a third grade level. He has never operated at a normal level, and he is in need of ongoing supervision due to his mental retardation. He continues to be confused and does not comprehend the proceedings against him. He is most anxious when discussing his pick-up by the police and going to the police station, as well as the nature of the charges and the attending events which have followed. It is my opinion that _____X_____ is not dangerous or lacking in adequate impulse controls. Furthermore, there is no past, or current, evidence of any outstanding sexual problems with him.

After having counselled with _____X_____ parents, in addition to the other aforementioned people, it is my professional opinion that no useful purpose would be served by changing the boy's environment or his routine. _____X_____ functions well under the supervision of his parents, both very aware people in this area. They have long-standing plans for his future and are consulting with me as to these plans.

I can only recommend to the court that _____ X _____ be permitted to remain with his parents, and that he is, and should continue to be, a useful, well-behaved, functioning member of society.

Respectfully,

Signature

www.ingramcontent.com/pod-product-compliance
Lightning Source LLC
Chambersburg PA
CBHW031314060726
47590CB00003B/1211